The Black Death

George Capaccio

Newbridge®

Before You Read

Imagine it's the year 1347. You are standing on the docks in a town in Italy. You watch excitedly as ships arrive with strange and marvelous goods from Asia. Now imagine your terror when you realize the ships have brought something else—a terrible plague called the Black Death! As you get ready to read this book, think about the following and take notes.

✠ Where have you read or heard about plagues?

✠ If you're sick, you go to a doctor or to the hospital. During the Middle Ages, there were no hospitals. There were a few doctors, but they had few ways to treat illness. What do you think you might have done if you got sick back then?

Preview the book by looking at the table of contents, headings, photos, and special features.

✠ What do you see in this book that you already know something about?

✠ List three facts or ideas you think you'll discover in this book.

✠ Look at the painting on pages 4 and 5. How do you think artwork like this can help you understand what life was like at the time of the plague?

✠ Write down two questions you have about the Black Death.

Contents

Life on a Manor

Who could have guessed that a terrifying death was on its way to millions? That a disaster worse than a war or a revolution was about to happen? It was the fourteenth century, during a period of history called the **Middle Ages.** Life in Europe was difficult then for many people. But no one expected how much harder it was about to get.

Life in the Country

Picture yourself waking up in England on a cold Sunday morning late in the year of 1348. Your bed is an old sack stuffed with straw. The tiny bedroom where your family sleeps is one of two cramped rooms in your hut. The walls are made with mud and sticks. The roof is thatched with straw. There's no chimney, so the room smells smoky. Your farm animals sleep in part of the house to help keep your family warm.

As you awaken, you remember that today your father has permission from the farm manager to go to town to sell part of the lord's harvest. You will be going, too.

Most people in the Middle Ages were peasants who lived on farms, just as their ancestors had for hundreds of years. Many peasants never left their farms in their entire lives.

You are already dressed in the same clothes you wear every day—a baggy, brown wool shirt, a pair of long wool stockings, and heavy wooden shoes. You eat a bowl of porridge and a large hunk of coarse, dark bread. Then you join your father outside. Your brothers will have chores to do all day, feeding the animals and bringing in the firewood. Your sisters will stay at home to weave cloth and mend clothes with your mother. They will have a little time to play later in the day, games like tag and hoops.

Your horse slowly pulls a two-wheeled wagon as you pass the pastures and fields that belong to the lord. His lands are called a **manor.** The lord of this manor owns not only the manor house overlooking these lands but the mill that grinds your grain, the oven that bakes your bread, all the sheep in the fields, and the forests and ponds nearby.

In England, most peasants like you and your father live on manors. You have freedom to own property and marry the person you choose. But you have to remain on the lord's manor. And you must work to take care of his fields and pastures. You get to keep the crops grown on your own fields, but you don't get paid for the hard work you do for the lord. You even have to pay to use the mill, the oven, and the

 Many manors in the Middle Ages were like small towns surrounded by the lord's lands. Some contained a mill, a church, fields, peasant huts, and a manor house, as shown on this map.

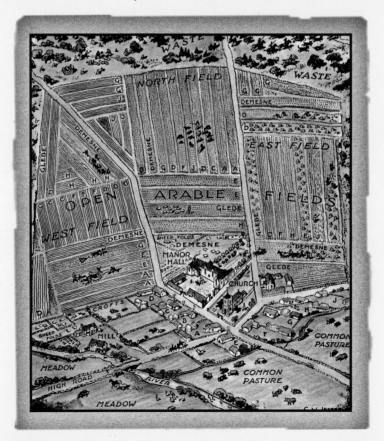

Stone masons, carpenters, skilled craftsmen, and shopkeepers lived inside the walls of crowded towns and cities. But most people in the Middle Ages were peasants who lived and worked on farms outside the walls.

lord's oxen that plow your fields. This is the only way of life you know. And this is the way life will go on unless some big changes take place.

Down the road you spot a peddler. He signals your father to stop. Then he holds up some carefully folded silks to sell. "I got them from a **merchant ship,**" he says. Your father doesn't stop. Lately, people avoid strangers—too many rumors about sailors dying on those merchant ships. And he can't afford silk anyway.

Just ahead, you pass the manor graveyard. Your grandparents, who lived and died on the manor, are buried there. So are the relatives of most of the people who live on the manor. You and your father remove your hats out of respect for the dead. Neither of you has any idea that in just a few months, half your village will be dead. The dead will include your mother and all but one of your brothers and sisters. And millions will be dead all over Europe.

The Death Ships

" Alas! our ships enter the
port, but of a thousand
sailors hardly ten are
spared. We reach our
homes; our kindred and
our neighbors come from
all parts to visit us. . . .
While we spoke to them,
while they embraced
us and kissed us, we
scattered the poison
from our lips."

Gabriele de' Mussi

As you bring your grain to market, people are already dying in Italy and France from a terrible disease. Here's how it happened. Without knowing it, overland traders and invaders from Central Asia carried the disease to Kaffa, a trading city on the Black Sea. When the disease began to spread through Kaffa, Italian sailors and traders who lived there fled the city. They headed back to Italy and other parts of Europe.

The Black Death Arrives

The ships headed for an Italian city called Messina. They were filled with Asian goods that people in Europe wanted—fine silks, spices, fancy dishes. But on this trip, the merchant ships carried something else no one wanted—sick sailors and passengers. And rats!

Within days, the deadly illness that had sickened and killed people in Kaffa began to infect many people on the ships. First they suffered high fevers and bone-deep pain. How awful it must have been, being trapped on those ships. People coughed, cried, and screamed constantly. The victims had lumps in their armpits and dark purple blotches on their skin. The smell of death was everywhere. The rotting bodies were simply tossed into the seas to clear the decks.

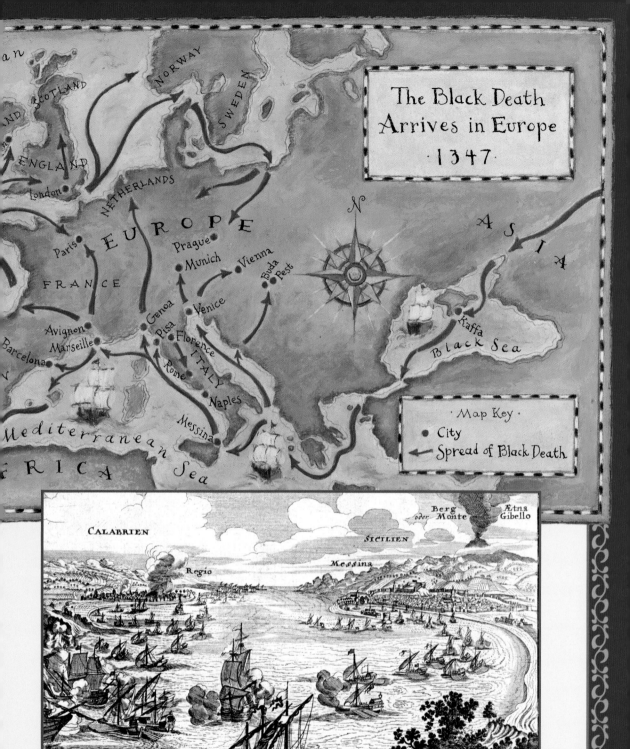

The Black Death
Arrives in Europe
·1347·

Map Key
• City
← Spread of Black Death

 People in Messina had no idea that millions had already died from the Black Death in Asia, where these ships had come from. Can you find Messina in this picture and on the map?

Meanwhile, the people of Messina went about their everyday lives. Fishermen brought in their catches. Peddlers sold their merchandise. And others stood on the docks ready to greet their loved ones on the ships coming in from Kaffa. None of these people knew that these would be their last normal days for years to come.

When the ships dropped their anchors, those onshore realized that something was terribly wrong. Only a handful of people got off. Black rats scurried down the ships' ropes or swam to shore. Those people who had eagerly awaited the passengers came face to face with the Black Death instead. For the ships from Kaffa brought home an unwelcome disease. It was a deadly, fast-spreading **plague** that killed its victims in a few days.

 Traders who traveled from Asia to Italy along a route called the Silk Road may have also carried the Black Death into Europe.

 Panicked people fled farms, villages, and towns to escape the Black Death. But there was no safe place to go.

Disease Escapes the Death Ships

Within days, officials in Messina ordered the ships to pull up their anchors and leave. But it was too late. The disease, carried by rats, had already left the ships and come ashore.

The ships sailed off to other ports in Europe. In this way, these ships and others from the Black Sea spread the plague. By land and by sea, the Black Death advanced like a tide into the rest of Europe.

Mashed Snakes and Bloodletting

People in Europe didn't know what had hit them. The disease that came off the Italian ships killed nearly every person it infected. Once on land, the plague spread from town to town and from country to country. Soon, the dead seemed to outnumber the living.

Fear and panic spread everywhere. People watched their families and friends die within days. In the cities, the streets were empty. Some people were too afraid to attend church or visit each other. In the countryside, some sick people left their homes to die in the woods so they wouldn't infect family members. Those who weren't sick didn't know if their own deaths would be next. The Black Death was destroying lives as much as starvation, war, or any natural disaster. How could people stop it?

 Even rich people couldn't escape death. During the Black Death and other plagues, like this one in 1630, everyone was affected. Death was often shown as skeletons in paintings.

12

Paid gravediggers picked up the dead bodies that families left in the street for burial. Sometimes a priest would say a quick prayer in the street for the dead.

Keeping the Plague Away

People grew desperate. The rich upper classes left crowded cities and villages. They hid in their country homes, away from others who might infect them. Most poor people stayed in their huts, where many sickened and died.

People depended on the few available doctors to tell them what to do. But doctors in the Middle Ages had no knowledge of how to treat or prevent a disease like this. They used the same cures that doctors had used for hundreds of years. These were no match for the Black Death. And religious laws prevented doctors from performing **autopsies** on the dead to learn more about the disease.

During the plague of 1720, just like the one in the Middle Ages, doctors wore strange face coverings and clothes to protect themselves.

Different Ideas About the Black Death

People living during the Middle Ages had never experienced a disease that killed so many so quickly. They were used to starvation, but this was different. Doctors and scientists didn't know what could cause such a deadly **epidemic.** With little scientific knowledge, people developed many ideas about the causes of the Black Death.

Ideas About What Caused It

- God was seeking revenge for people's sinful behavior.
- The air was poisoned.
- A flying "Pest Maiden" on a blue flame waved a red scarf to spread the disease.
- The unusual way the planets lined up caused a poisonous cloud to rise over the Earth.
- An imbalance of fluids formed in a person's body.
- Clothing that people wore carried the disease.

 People burned the clothes and houses of the dead. Some kept fires going because they believed smoke would keep away poisoned air.

People tried all kinds of treatments to avoid the disease or to cure it once a victim became sick. Some of these treatments may seem unusual to us today, but they made sense to the people at the time.

Ideas About How to Avoid or to Treat It

✠ Place live leeches on the patient's body to suck out bad blood.
✠ Recite magic words.
✠ Feed the patient a medicine of mashed snake meat.
✠ Have the patient pray all the time.
✠ Avoid giving the patient a bath so "bad air" doesn't enter the skin.
✠ Prepare homemade herbal brews for the patient to drink.
✠ Sit in a room surrounded by burning **incense.**

Bloodletting, or using leeches to suck blood from patients, was a common treatment for many illnesses, including the plague, during the Middle Ages.

Some people tried strange recipes for medicines and **potions** to prevent or cure the Black Death.

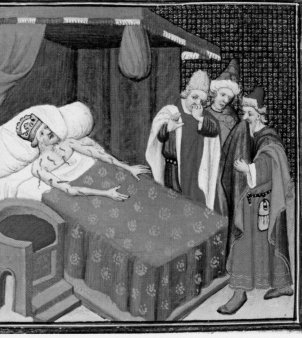

Death on Every Doorstep

Six months have passed. After your mother died, your brothers and sisters died one by one, until the only people left were you, your father, and your youngest sister. Half your village died. And it was like this in most of Europe. When the Black Death first hit, in 1347, there may have been more than 80 million people in Europe. Four years later, the epidemic had killed almost one-third of Europe's population. Imagine what life would be like today if one out of every three people died within a few days. In many cases, whole villages died. That's how terrifying this disease was.

Before the Black Death, most funerals were peaceful and respectful. Families helped bury their loved ones in coffins, or they carried them to the cemetery.

Beliefs About Death

Before the epidemic, Europeans accepted death as a natural part of living. People followed Catholic death **rituals** in most parts of Europe. Friends and relatives would stand watch over the body all night, then carry the **corpse** on their shoulders to the burial place in a nearby church cemetery. The village priest would perform prayers and say **mass.** These rituals reminded people how important each life was.

Many artists painted death as a skeleton during the epidemic. They showed Death as a figure who could enter a room at any time, like a friend or loved one.

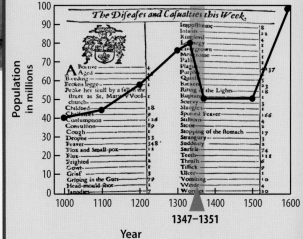

Effect of the Black Death on Europe's Population

During the plague, though, these death customs changed. Some priests were unwilling to carry out their duties. They were afraid of getting sick and dying. Many did. Relatives were left to drag the corpses of their loved ones out of their homes and leave them on doorsteps. Some of the poor made a living by hauling the corpses to mass graves where hundreds of bodies were buried. The workers would quickly cover the bodies with dirt and return to town for the next load.

Living with Death

Death affected the living in different ways. On the Italian island of Sicily, where the epidemic first hit, **archaeologists** found bodies buried where they had died, far from villages and towns. People may have left their homes and estates in panic. They probably didn't want to infect their loved ones.

Some people locked themselves indoors until the plague passed. Others tried not to think about it. They drank in taverns and refused to talk about all the sickness around them. In Venice, Italy, authorities finally shut down taverns to keep order. There, special burial boats carried the dead out to deserted islands. They were buried in proper, individual graves, with a priest saying a prayer over each body.

 Prayer, not panic, helped some people cope with the horrors of the Black Death.

In England, villages and city neighborhoods lost huge numbers of people. Even today, visitors can see the ruins of villages that emptied out during the time of the Black Death. Archaeologists have discovered plague pits where bodies were carefully wrapped in cloth and buried in rows. Some records show that criminals stole from the houses of the dead. Other records describe people in places all over England who kept order. They kept life going even in the middle of so much death.

 Artists painted images of the Dance of Death on church and graveyard walls after the Black Death and other epidemics. Such images reminded the living that death could return again and again, even while people were dancing and singing.

Life After the Black Death

> " You might see villas [country homes] or fortified places lately filled with crowds of men, and on the next day, all had departed and everything was in utter silence. "
>
> Matteo Villani

Although you, your father, and your sister have survived the plague, the disease has killed your old way of life. You find yourselves looking at empty huts and barns, overgrown fields, and wandering animals.

With few survivors from your village, there aren't enough people to tend the lord's fields or watch his animals.

Soon you and your lord realize the same thing: He needs you more than you need him. Like other surviving peasants, you and your father demand to get paid for your work. With money, you can rent or buy some of the lord's lands to grow more crops.

 Before the plague, peasants bought goods on **credit** from shopkeepers, which they paid back with part of their harvest of crops. After the Black Death, peasants began to use money to pay for goods.

As you look around, you see other survivors on the move. Gradually, those who are still alive realize they are no longer tied to the manors where they were born.

Of course, the lords fight to keep their old way of life. They pass laws to keep peasants from leaving the manors. But the laws fail. Workers want to own land or make more money. Many lords and workshop owners have to give in to these demands. Most of them begin to pay workers like you and your family good money to work for them.

As a plague survivor, you have lived through months of horror. You have lost so much—family, relatives, neighbors, friends, and the protection of the lords. But you have gained something too—your freedom to live and work where you want.

By the time the Black Death was over, many castles and manor houses stood empty.

A New Class of People

One of the most important changes that took place at the end of the plague was the rise of a **middle class** in Europe. Before the plague, most Europeans had been either very rich or very poor. The rich upper class had all the money, power, and property. The poor lower classes worked as farmers on the manors or as laborers in the towns and cities.

Once poorer people received **wages,** a middle class developed. And with higher and higher wages, the poor got a taste of what it was like to have money, power, and freedom. Some peasants who stayed in the countryside used their wages to rent or buy land to grow their own crops. Peasants even wore the expensive clothes of the dead lords and ladies. Here's what the writer Matteo Villani noticed about this new middle class: "The common people . . . would no longer work at

 For centuries before the Black Death, peasants wore simple **homespun** clothes made of coarse sheep's wool that women wove at home.

 Once they earned more money, the new middle class demanded fancy clothes they couldn't make at home. Workshops increased the production of fine fabrics in fancy colors. These had to be woven on new, improved machines.

their . . . trades; they wanted the dearest and most delicate food . . . while children and common women clad [dressed] themselves in all the fair and costly garments [clothes] of the illustrious who had died."

When the plague was over, many peasants moved their families to big cities. There, some joined **guilds,** or workers' groups, to become skilled **craftsmen,** such as glassmakers, silversmiths, shoemakers, and guild merchants.

 People turned to private prayer at home after the Black Death left many churches without priests.

A Different World

Freedom opened up new possibilities in many areas of life. The church changed. Younger, inexperienced priests replaced many of the church leaders of the past. People didn't depend as much on these new priests to tell them how to pray or live their lives.

New Ways of Learning

Education changed. Before the Black Death, most books were written in Latin. Few people knew how to read. Even university classes were taught in Latin. After the Black Death, books written in everyday languages like English, French, German, and Italian became more and more common. Because the middle classes and even peasants had more money after the Black Death, they were able to hire schoolmasters to teach their children how to read and write. Some of them even went on to universities. Knowledge of literature, science, and mathematics spread through the population.

Johannes Gutenberg invented the printing press in the 1450s. Books could be produced cheaply, so more people could afford to buy them.

New Ways of Working

With fewer people willing to do farm work, landowners had to change the way they used their land. Some completely stopped farming their fields. Others **leased,** or rented, their part of their farmlands to peasants. Still others switched from farming to sheep raising, which required less labor. And many landowners found ways to work more efficiently. They used more labor-saving machines, such as windmills and watermills.

Middle-class workers were busy with their jobs. They had less time to weave their

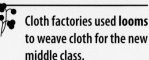
Cloth factories used **looms** to weave cloth for the new middle class.

 Windmills now did the work of pumping water and grinding grain that peasants had once done by hand.

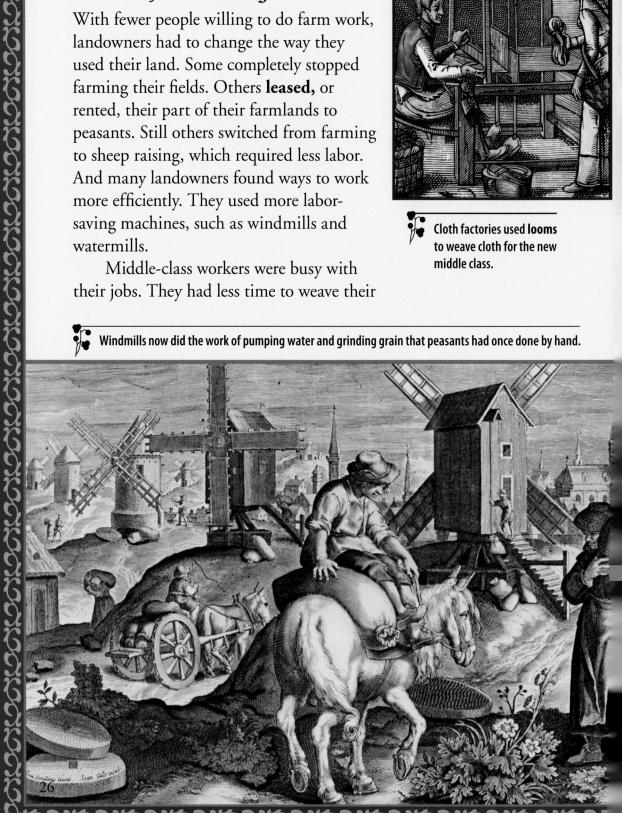

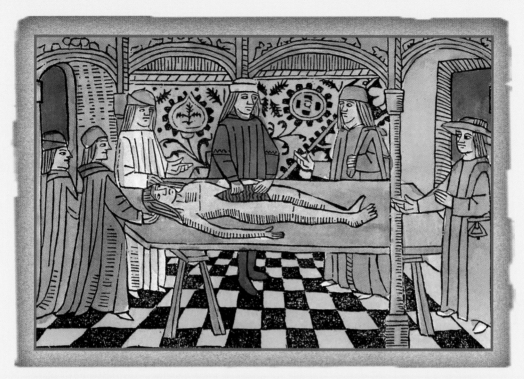

 Doctors learned more about the inside of the human body through **surgery** and autopsies.

own cloth. New clothing industries developed. Silk and linen became more available than they had been in the past. Some workshops took rough fabrics from other countries and improved them to make finer cloth.

New Medical Practices

Doctors now studied **anatomy** to learn more about the organs and other structures inside the human body. Some doctors even treated diseases by operating on patients with more sophisticated techniques than before the Black Death.

After the Black Death, the Catholic Church allowed doctors to perform autopsies on corpses. Once doctors could see inside the human body, they gained a better understanding of how the body worked and how diseases affected it. A new interest in **public health** and the importance of **hygiene** began. Still, it took another five hundred years before the real cause of the Black Death would be discovered.

Plagues Through the Ages

What actually caused the Black Death that killed so many people in the Middle Ages and again throughout the centuries? Has the disease disappeared for good?

In 1894, the plague broke out in the city of Hong Kong, China. At the time, a scientist named Alexandre Yersin was studying the disease in Indochina. He was sent to China to find its cause. Yersin examined body tissue that came from corpses with a powerful microscope. That's when he discovered the deadly **bacteria** that caused the plague. In the same year,

Rats!

Rat bites don't cause plagues. Flea bites do. Fleas prefer living on **host** animals like black rats that carry the fleas on them. When a rat dies, the plague-infected flea looks for a new host, sometimes a human. Alexander Yersin may have been the first person to make the connection between plague, rats, and fleas.

Plague Epidemics, 1347–Present

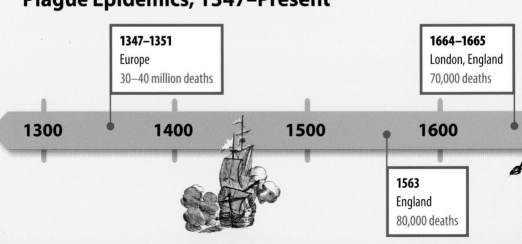

1347–1351
Europe
30–40 million deaths

1664–1665
London, England
70,000 deaths

1300   1400   1500   1600

1563
England
80,000 deaths

a Japanese doctor, Kitasato Shibasaburo, made the same discovery. Both men realized that these bacteria live in the bellies of fleas. The fleas travel on rats, and people get the disease when they are bitten by the infected fleas.

Alexandre Yersin

More Than One Kind of Plague

Since 1894, scientists have discovered three forms of the plague. They still aren't sure if just one kind of "super" plague was the killer in 1347–1351. Some scientists aren't even certain that flea-carrying rats were responsible for the plague. But many experts believe that the Black Death quickly turned into a more deadly disease that traveled through the air and attacked people's lungs. It then spread from person to person.

Scientists named the Black Death the **bubonic plague.** That's because victims develop strange, egg-shaped lumps called **buboes.** Doctors now treat the disease with **antibiotics.** These medicines usually cure the killer disease if it's caught in time.

You can still see the effects of the Black Death that arrived in Europe in 1347. . . in ruined villages, old graveyards, famous paintings, and the written memories of those who lived through it, like Matteo Villani. He wrote: ". . . You might see the world brought back to its ancient silence. . . . There were no footsteps of passersby, no murderer was seen, yet the corpses of the dead were more than the eye could discern [see clearly]. . . ."

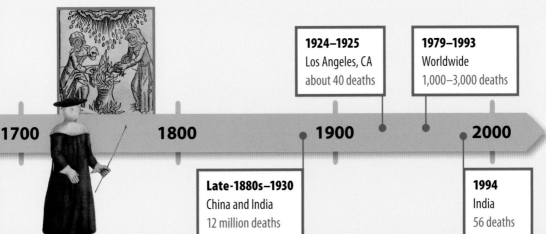

1924–1925
Los Angeles, CA
about 40 deaths

1979–1993
Worldwide
1,000–3,000 deaths

1700   1800   1900   2000

Late-1880s–1930
China and India
12 million deaths

1994
India
56 deaths

Keep Going!

Here are some ways to share what you've learned, find out more, and develop your talents. Maybe you'll come up with your own idea.

Think and Write

✠ Think about the effects of the Black Death on Europe in the 1300s. Now imagine that a third of our population (about 100 million people) were killed by a modern plague. Think how the effects might be similar to and different from those of the Black Death. Give your answers in a paragraph or two.

Dig Deeper

✠ What questions that you had before you read the book are still unanswered? What new questions came up in reading? You can start looking for answers at these Websites. When you find them, write them down and tell where you found them.

Middle Ages
www.learner.org/exhibits/middleages

The Black Death, 1348
www.eyewitnesstohistory.com/plague.htm

Talk with Experts

✠ Division of Vector-Borne Infections of the National Center for Infectious Diseases:
www.cdc.gov/ncidod/dvbid/misc/mission.htm
It's part of the huge U.S. government's Centers for Disease Control (CDC). Click on the "Plague" listing to find out about bubonic plague in the world today.

✠ At U.S. Doctors for Africa,
www.usdoctorsforafrica.org
you can find out how doctors from our country are helping people with HIV/AIDS in Africa, where the disease is widespread.

Medicine Through the Ages

✠ When the Black Death killed millions of people in Europe in the 1300s, they didn't know what hit them. Since then, we have learned a great deal about diseases, their causes, and their cures. Choose an important discovery in the treatment of disease. Some ideas are: the microscope, animals that carry disease, vaccines, germs, and antibiotics. Prepare a short report or presentation (poster, diorama, computer slide show, etc.) on how the discovery changed the world.

Glossary

anatomy \ə na′ tə mē\ *n.* the study of the organs and structures of the body

antibiotic \an tē bī ä′ tik\ *n.* a medicine that destroys germs

archaeologist \är kē ä′ lə jist\ *n.* a person who studies the remains of ancient cultures

autopsy \ô′ täp sē\ *n.* surgery on a body to study the cause of death

bacteria \bak tir′ ē ə\ *n.* a group of microscopic organisms that live in water, plants, animals, or soil. They sometimes cause disease.

bloodletting \bləd′ le tiŋ\ *n.* the removal of some of a patient's blood for the treatment of a disease

bubo \byü′ bō\ *n.* a swollen, infected lump on the body

bubonic plague \byü bä′ nik plāg\ *n.* a deadly disease caused by fleas carried by rats

corpse \korps\ *n.* a dead body

craftsman \krafts′ mən\ *n.* a skilled worker

credit \kre′ dit\ *n.* money lent to an individual or group to buy goods

epidemic \e pə de′ mik\ *n.* a sudden outbreak of a disease affecting a large population

guild \gild\ *n.* an organized group of skilled workers

homespun \hōm′ spən\ *adj.* woven at home

host \hōst\ *n.* a living animal that provides a home to another living thing

hygiene \hī′ jēn\ *n.* the science of staying healthy

incense \in′ sents\ *n.* a material that makes a pleasant smell when it is burned

lease \lēs\ *v.* rent land for an amount of time

loom \lüm\ *n.* a machine for weaving cloth

manor \ma′ nər\ *n.* a large home and its lands

mass \mas\ *n.* a religious ceremony in a church; *adj.* involving a large quantity

merchant ship \mər′ chənt ship\ *n.* a trading ship

Middle Ages \mi′ dəl ā′ jəz\ *n.* a period of time in Europe between AD 500 and 1500

middle class \mi′ dəl klas\ *n.* a social and economic group between the upper and lower classes

plague \plāg\ *n.* a deadly disease that affects many people

potion \pō′ shən\ *n.* a mix of liquids

public health \pə′ blik helth\ *n.* the protection of the health of a community

ritual \ri′ chə wəl\ *n.* a ceremony performed in a specific way

surgery \sər′ jə rē\ *n.* a branch of medicine that treats diseases and conditions with operations

wage \wāj\ *n.* a payment for work

Pronunciation Key

\ə\ **a**mong \ər\ m**u**rder \a\ **a**sk \ā\ **a**pe \ä\ h**o**p, c**a**r \ch\ **ch**op \e\ **e**nd \ē\ gr**ea**sy \g\ **g**et \i\ h**i**d \ī\ **i**ce \j\ **j**et \ŋ\ ki**ng** \ō\ n**o** \ô\ s**a**w \oi\ t**oy** \oo\ b**oo**k \ou\ **ou**t \th\ **th**ank \th\ **th**en \ü\ b**oo**t \y\ **y**ou \zh\ A**s**ian

Index